Hacking

By: PG WIZARD BOOKS

Top Online Handbook in Exploitation of Computer Hacking, Security, and Penetration Testing!

Hacking: Top Online Handbook in Exploitation of Computer Hacking, Security, and Penetration Testing!

Hacking: Top Online Handbook in Exploitation of Computer Hacking, Security, and Penetration Testing!

Table of Contents

Introduction

The world of hacking is an interesting world. Most of us only understand what is going on based on the movies that we watch or the news that we read about hackers stealing identities of those around them. These are parts of the whole hacking world, but there is so much more that comes with it. For example, some hackers are considered ethical hackers, which means that they are going to work to prevent others from getting onto their own systems, or the systems of others they are working for.

This guidebook is going to take some time to discuss the basics of the hacking world. We will start out with the difference between white hat hackers and black hat hackers and how each of them are going to work on the hacks that they are creating. We will then move on to working with how to map out your hack, especially if you want to check for vulnerabilities inside of your own system. And then the rest of the book will spend time looking at some of the common types of hacking that you can do including man in the middle hacks and even hacking passwords.

Even when it comes to hacking into a network that you are allowed to be on, it is important to learn how to do some basic hacks because you will be using the same methods that the black hat hackers are doing as well. This guidebook is going to help you to get started with doing some of the hacks that you need to ensure that you are getting the best results that you want!

Chapter 1: Some of the Basics of Computer Hacking

The process of hacking has gotten a bad name, mainly because of all the stories that have gone on in the media and in the movies about this topic. We may imagine someone who is just trying to get onto a system the are not allowed to be in or about someone who hacks into the government computers in order to get some important information and save the day. But there are many different facets that come up when we are talking about hacking and while some hackers are interested in stealing information and being places they aren't allowed to be, there are some who are more interested in learning hacking in order to protect their own computer systems and information.

There are two main types of computer hacking that you can come across. These include:

- Black hat hacking: this is the type that is found inside the movies. This is when someone tries to get onto a system that they don't belong, without the permission of the person who owns the system. Often this is done so that the hacker is able to get information they are not supposed to have, such as your personal information and credit card numbers.
- White hat hacking: this is the type of hacking that you may do when trying to keep your computer system and information safe from someone who may try to get the information and use it for their own reasons. Also, white hat hackers may also work with a big company, working on hacking on the system to see if it is vulnerable, in order to keep other people out of the system.

Both of these types of hackers are going to use the same methods to do the hacking, but the reasons behind the hacking are going to be completely different. It is important to note that black hat hacking is illegal and if you do this kind of hacking, it could end up with you going to jail and in a lot of trouble. But there is nothing wrong with hacking on to a system that you have permission to be on, such as your own personal computer, to help keep it safe or as part of your job.

Hacking: Top Online Handbook in Exploitation of Computer Hacking, Security, and Penetration Testing!

Penetration testing

Now that we have a little basics of the world of hacking, it is time to look more into the world of computer hacking. We will start this out with penetration testing. This is known as an authorized attempt in order to exploit a computer system in the hopes of learning the flaws that are inside of it so that you can work to make it more secure. When you are given the assignment to do a penetration test, or you decide to do it on your own system, you will be investigating the system in order to prove that there are vulnerabilities in the network.

After you are done with doing the penetration test, the mitigation measures will be made in order to address any of the issues that you found and fix the issues that you discovered during this test. It is basically a process of finding the threats that are present inside of the system and then come up with a good plan that is going to take care of the issues that show up during the test. Doing these on occasion to the system can ensure that you catch the vulnerabilities inside the system before someone else gets on and steals your information.

Penetration testing is also known as ethical hacking. There is a very thin line that is present between vulnerability assessment and penetration testing. These terms are often interchanged but they are not really the same thing. For example, the vulnerability assessment is going to be responsible for evaluations the system for any security issues that may be present already. But the penetration test is going to be the test that is used in order to exploit and also proves that these security issues exist. The test is going to allow the hacker to test out the system as an outside source so that they can see how the vulnerabilities are affecting things.

As a white hat hacker, you would want to go through the system and perform the same actions that a black hat hacker would do on the system in this kind of test. You would try to get onto the system to see how bad the vulnerabilities are and to determine what information others are able to see. While the black hat hacker would simply do this in the hopes of trying to get onto the system and exploit it for their own personal gains, you are going to find out where these things are and learn how to close them up. Even though both of you will use the same methods in order to get onto the system, you are going to have different reasons for getting onto the system.

Hacking: Top Online Handbook in Exploitation of Computer Hacking, Security, and Penetration Testing!

A hacking lab

As a beginner to working on hacking, you may want to consider working in a hacking lab. This is a safe environment that you are able to work in with the attacks and the traffic to see how they respond to different things that you are working on, without them getting out of hand and heading to places they are not supposed to be. This is a good place for a beginner to get started with because it allows you to get some practice without ruining anything in the system or causing some issues. Once you get a little bit more of the practice into the thing, you will be able to move out of the hacking lab and have some fun with hacking, and do some of the tests, on a real network.

While there are some differences in the reason for hacking between a white hat and a black hat hacker, both of these groups are going to use the same kinds of skills and techniques in order to get the information that they want. The trick here is for the white hat hacker to know just as much, of not more, and to be faster at finding the vulnerabilities compared to the black hat hacker. This will help to keep the system protected and ensures that the other group isn't able to get information they are not supposed to have.

Chapter 2: Mapping Out the Hack Before Beginning

So before we get too far in this process, it is important to come up with the plan that you want to use. This is meant to give you a good idea of what you need to do and where you want to look for some of these vulnerabilities inside of your system. The strategies that you will use are important, but you really need to focus on having a good plan in place before you get too far in this process.

When you are trying to find some of the vulnerabilities that are needed, you don't need to waste your time checking all of the protocols for security at the same time. This can make it a bit confusing and sometimes it is going to make you deal with more problems than you want because too much information is coming towards you. This means that you should break your system up into parts and then test each of these parts so that the work is more manageable overall.

For the most part, it is a good idea to start out with the application or system that you are worried about the most, and then go down the list until you get to each of them. To help you to determine which of the systems you should work with first, consider these questions:

- If the system is attacked, which system or application is going to cause the most issues. Which one has the most information or would be the hardest to fix up if it were lost.
- If the system is attacked, which application is going to be the easiest for the hacker to get in to.
- Which sections of the system are you working on and are considered the least documented, which means that they are rarely checked. Do you notice some that you have never seen there before?

As you answer these questions, it is going to become easier to figure out which applications you should work on first and it is easier to go through the whole process and find the results that you want. There are many places that you are able to check out to make sure the tests are run the proper way including the routers and the switches, workstations and laptops, operating systems, databases and applications, firewalls, files, and emails servers and more. It is possible that you will need to run many tests to get all of these so take your time and try them out to see where the vulnerabilities may lie.

When should I do my hack?

Once you have a good list of the applications and devices that you want to check, the next question that you may have is when is a good time to hack. You will need to make sure that you complete the hacks during a time that is going to cause the least amount of disruption in the company or on your own personal computer. This means during the peak hours of the day, you should not be doing these hacks because they could potentially cause a lot of slow down and issues with the system and depending on the type of hack that you do, and if it goes well or not, it could even shut down the network when it is needed most. The best time to complete the tasks is when there is going to be minimal disruption, so coming in after hours is often best since few people will be on the system or the building could be closed and no one will even notice.

The time that works the best for these hacks will vary depending on the situation. For example, if you are doing one of these hacks on your own computer, the timing may not matter as much because you would just pick a time when you are free to do the hacks and call it good. On the other hand, if you are doing this as a job for your employer, you will need to abide by their busy times and pick one that is not going to interfere with the business, especially if the hack does cause some issues.

Will others see what I am doing?

When you are working on these hacks in order to find some of the vulnerabilities that are in the system, you need to think just like a criminal hacker would, since these are the type of people that would try to get onto the system. Sometimes being able to look at the system through fresh eyes can make all the difference. For example, when you are used to using this system, you are an insider and could have troubles seeing what is going on in the system, but it is important that you make sure that when you do the hacks, no one else is able to see what you are doing. The criminal hacker would be careful about who is able to notice their presence so you would want to be the same way.

Hacking: Top Online Handbook in Exploitation of Computer Hacking, Security, and Penetration Testing!

Now, it is your job to also check out what the hacker is able to see on your system. Hackers are always trying to find out as much information about the system as possible to make it easier to get onto it, and there are trails left all over the place for them to look at. As the ethical hacker of the system, it is your responsibility to find out what kind of information is out there for the other hackers to find and then learn how to diminish these trails to make your website and system harder to mess with. There are several different scanner types that you are able to use, such as a port scanner, so that you can see what information that is being shared, making it easier to catch some of these issues. Some of the other searches that you can do to protect your network includes doing a search online for the following information:

Any contact details. This is going to be information that can point back to the people connected with your business. Some options like USSearch and ChoicePoint are good ones to visit and see if your information is present there.

Look for any recent press releases that may talk about changes that have happened in the organization.

Look through any of the acquisitions and mergers of the company.

Always see if you can find any SEC documents about the company online.

Any patents or trademarks that are associated with this company.

Incorporation filings. These are also found through the SEC, but sometimes they are located elsewhere.

Be as thorough as possible about this point so that you have a good idea of what hackers are able to find out about your company or about your network. Often doing a keyword search is not going to bring up the results that you would like so you need to work with some advanced searches to find out all the information that you would like. At this point, you have a good idea of the different things that your computer or your network is sending out to other people and you can create the plan to get it all under control. Deleting information from online can help but running some port and network scans are great as well. Go through as many of these scans and tests as you can to help keep the computer network as safe as possible.

Chapter 3: Doing a Spoofing Attack

The first type of attack that we are going to explore is the spoofing attack. Whether you are working as a criminal hacker or as an ethical hacker, there are a lot of things that you can work with in order to get into a system that you shouldn't be on. As a hacker, you are responsible for researching and having some patience to wait in order to find the vulnerability that is on the system or network before taking the next move. But with the right kind of work, it is easier to get on the network and often a few different options are going to show up for you. One method that you can use is the spoofing technique that allows you to convince the computer system that you should be there so that you can get all the information that you want. Let's take a look at how this works and how you can make it happen with your hacking.

Spoofing

One of the first techniques that we are going to explore in this guidebook is spoofing. This is basically going to be a technique where the hacker is able to pretend that they are another person, software, website, or organization in order to convince the network that they are supposed to be here. The hacker is meant to look like this other person so that the network will allow them through the security protocols and then the hacker can get through where they want, get the information that is needed, and even leave the system before anyone else is able to see them. There are a few options that you are able to pick from when it comes to the spoofing technique including:

IP spoofing

With the technique of IP spoofing, the hacker is going to mask up their IP address or make changes to it so that the network things that the hacker belongs to the network. The hacker is able to make these changes so that the IP address either matches up with what is allowed on the network or it is one that the network is going to be familiar with. With this method, the hacker is able to be in any part of the world that they want, but the network is still going to allow them to get on because the IP address matches up in some manner. Once the hacker is able to get on to the system, they have the ability to take over this network, change files, delete things, and do some other tasks without ever being detected.

11

If the hacker is able to pull off this technique, it is very successful because it has convinced the network that the hacker is supposed to be there. The trusted IP address is found by the hacker and then it is used to get onto the network and make the changes that are needed. The hacker will be able to use this in order to gain full access to the whole system, whether they choose to sit around and wait for a good opportunity or they choose to do an attack and get the information they want right away.

DNS spoofing

Another spoofing technique is known as DNS spoofing. This method is going to trick a user who is trying to get onto a legitimate site. The hacker will take the IP address and then when a user clicks on it, they will be sent to a malicious website where the hacker has complete control. Sometimes the hacker will take over a legitimate website and turn it to their use, but often they will change around a letter or two to trick people. Users who aren't paying attention or who type in the address wrong will be sent to a bad website and the hacker can take credentials and private information from the user.

Often the user will not realize that they are being tricked. They will get onto the website and figure that it is just where they want to be. They can put in private information, send payment, and more while the hacker is collecting it all privately.

For the hacker to get this to work, they need to have the same LAN as their target. This requires the hacker to search for a weak password on one of the machines that is on the network, something that is possibly even from a different location. Once the hacker accomplishes this, they will be able to redirect all users to their website and easily monitor the activities that are done there.

Email spoofing

Email spoofing is one of the most common types of spoofing, which is one of the reasons that people should be very careful about the emails that they are receiving, sending, and clicking on. This can be a useful technique when the hacker wants to try and get past some of the security that is placed on email accounts. Most email servers are going to be good at recognizing if someone looks like they are legitimate and when something is spam, but there are also times when the hacker will be able to get past this and can send malicious attachments.

The most common form of this is when the hacker is able to pretend to be someone else inside the system so that they can intercept the emails from both parties, either read them or make changes, and then send the emails on without either of the two parties knowing. This can be really useful to the hacker because they can really get stuff done, and get ahold of private information that might be hidden elsewhere.

Phone number spoofing

When it comes to using phone number spoofing, the hacker is going to get ahold of some false numbers, or even area codes, so that they can mask their location. This is the best way for the hacker to be able to get into some of the voicemail messages that you have, and even to send out some text messages using this number. The target is often misled about where the hacker is from. Often this one is used when the hacker wants to pretend that they belong to a government office to trick the target.

The spoofing attacks can be difficult because often the network administrator is not even able to find out these attacks. The hacker will be able to stay on the network and cause almost as much damage as they want to these systems, without ever being found. It is often only after the hacker causes a big mess or when important information is leaked out that the hacker is finally caught and taken off the system. The hacker will be able to use just these kinds of hacks or some of the others in order to get the results they want and often they will be undetected by others on the same network.

Chapter 4: Man in the Middle Attacks

In addition to being able to do the spoofing attacks that we talked about in the previous chapter, it is also possible for a hacker to do a man in the middle attack. Sometimes the hacker will do this as a passive attack in order to just get on the system and see what information they are able to get, and other times they will use an active attack to get information, slow down the system, or cause some other form of problems.

When it comes to the man in the middle attacks, the hacker is able to do this with a form of spoofing that is called Address Resolution Protocol, or ARP. With this, the hacker is able to send messages that are false, but which are going to look normal, all over the network that they are working on. When it is pulled off, these fake messages allow the hacker to link up with another IP address of one of the users on the network. Once the hacker is done with this part, they can receive any of the data that all of the users are sending with this IP address and use it in the way that they would like.

So basically with this, the hacker is taking over an IP address and making it their own. They will receive all files, communication, and other information that is meant to go to the original user and they can use it however they would like. The hacker has the ability to get onto the network while receiving all traffic that goes on the network as well.

1. Session hijacking—this is when the hacker will use their false ARP to still the user's ID for the session. The hacker will be able to hold on to the information about the traffic and use it at a later date to get access to the account.

2. Denial of service attack—this is an attack done when the ARP spoof links several IP addresses to the target. During this attack, the data that should be sent to the other IP addresses are sent to one device. This is going to result in an overload of data.

3. Man in the middle attack—with this attack, the hacker is going to pretend that they are non-existent inside the network. Since they are hidden, they are able to modify and intercept messages that are sent between two or more users on the network. The one network may send a legitimate email, but the hacker will take it and change the information to be more

malicious before sending it on. The second user will open the malicious information, believing it to be safe.

Now that we know a bit more about a man in the middle attack, you are probably interested in learning some of the steps that are needed in order to complete the man in the middle attack. Here are some of the options that you can use and we are going to bring in the tool called Backtrack in order to get this done:

Do the research

The first step that you will need to do is find out the data that is needed to begin. The tool Wireshark is a good one to work with because it will help you to get all of this information to get on to the system. Firing up this tool on the network is going to allow the hacker to see what traffic is able to get onto the network through either the wireless or wired networks and is a really good place to get started for an access point.

Use your wireless adapter in monitor mode

Now that we have done some research, it is time to work with the wireless adapter and change it over to what is known as the monitor mode. This mode is going to make it easier for you to see the traffic that goes into your connection, even the traffic that isn't allowed to be there. This method is the one that you will work when using hubbed networks because you will find that the hubbed ones won't have as much security as you will find with the switched networks.

If you are able to see what information is going between the users that are on the switch, or you would like to make a bypass over this completely, you are able to work on making changes to the entries that are inside of your CAM table that is responsible for mapping out the IP and MAC addresses that are sending information to each other. When you are able to make changes to these entries, it is easier to get ahold of this traffic, make changes or at least read through it, and then send it back on without others knowing. The ARP spoofing attack is going to make this easier to accomplish.

Turning on backtrack

Now that you have changed the adapter and gotten it set up the way that you would like, it is time to fire up the Backtrack that you would like to use. You will need to pull up the Backtrack and then pull up all three terminals. Next, you will replace the MAC address from the target client with your personal MAC address. The code for doing this is: arpspoof [client IP] [server IP].

Once you do that, you will need to reverse the order of the IP addresses in the string that you just used. This is going to tell the server that your computer is the authorized one so that you are allowed to get onto the system and perform other tasks. You are basically going to become the server and the client so you can

15

receive packets of information and change them how you wish. It also goes the other way around.

For those who are using Linux, you can use the built in feature known as ip_forward, which will make it easier to forward the packets you are receiving. Once you turn this feature on, you will be able to go back into Backtrack and forward these packets with the commandecho 1 >/proc/sys/net/ipv4/ip_forward.

This command is going to make it easier to be right between the client and the server. You will get all the information that goes between these two and as the hacker, you can use the information as you wish. You could look at the system, take personal information, or change anything you want about information that is shared.

Check out your traffic

At this point, you should be able to get access to all of the information that the users are all sending through the network. You will get to be right in the front row of this action and you can either watch the information that is being sent or grab ahold of some of it and make changes before sending it all back through the system again. You can use your BackTrack tool in order to sniff out the traffic and get a nice clear picture of the system. You need to take some time to activate this feature in order to make it work, but it can make things easier to work with.

Get your data as well as the credentials

Now you will just need to wait around and see when the client is logging into the server. Once the client logs on, you will be able to see their username and password coming up right in front of you. This means that the information is going to be right in front of you, making it easier to record and use it whenever you would like. Since the users and the administrators are all going to use these same credentials on all of the systems on the computer, you can keep using these credentials in order to get anywhere that you would like. You are now right in the middle of all the information on the system and you can use it in any manner that you would like, without other users on the system having any idea.

And now you are done creating your very first man in the middle attack. This is a great way for you to get in the middle of the all the action on a system, and the other users will have no idea that you are there. There are many things that you are able to do from here, such as intercepting information, changing the messages that are sent, slowing down the system, and even getting ahold of some classified information. this can really put the hacker right in the middle of the action so it is a great way for you to get started.

Hacking: Top Online Handbook in Exploitation of Computer Hacking, Security, and Penetration Testing!

Chapter 5: How to Use Hacking to Get Passwords

The biggest target of hackers is to get passwords, mainly because they are really easy to get. Most people think that they just need to come up with a longer password in order to protect themselves, but there is more to it than that. If the hacker is able to use some of the tricks we stated earlier in this chapter, it does not matter how long your username and password is, they will still have it sent directly to them.

Confidential log in information, including passwords, are considered the weakest links in security because the only thing it relies on is secrecy. Once the secret is out, the security is pretty much gone. This is why it is such a big deal when a big company is hacked and all the username and passwords are leaked. The hacker is now able to get onto the system and use your information however they wish. Sometimes, the user themselves will inadvertently give out their own password for hackers to use.

So how do you hack a password? There are several ways that the hacker can do this including a physical attack, social engineering, and inference. There are also a few different tools that are used to crack passwords including:

1. Cain and Abel—this one is good to help with Windows RDP passwords, Cisco IOS hashes and more.

2. Elmcomsoft Distributed Password Recovery—this one is able to get PGP and Microsoft Office passwords and has been used in order to crack distributed passwords as well as recover up to 10,000 networked computers.

3. Elmcomsoft System Recovery—this has the ability to set administrative credentials, rest expirations on passwords, and reset passwords on Windows computers.

4. Ophcrack—this will use rainbow tables to crack passwords for Windows.

5. Pandora—this can be a good one to use to crack Novell Netware accounts either online or offline.

Some of these tools do have a shortfall because they will require the hacker to have physical access to the system they are hacking. But once the hacker has access to the system that you are protecting, they will be able to dig into all of your encrypted and password protected files with just a few tools.

Hacking: Top Online Handbook in Exploitation of Computer Hacking, Security, and Penetration Testing!

Often, the hacker is not going to have access to your computer to do a password hack and they will rely on some other tools. Some examples of other methods used to hack a password include:

1. Dictionary attacks—these are attacks that will make use of dictionary words against the password database. This makes it easier to figure out if there is a weak password in the system.

2. Brute force attacks—these are capable of cracking all types of passwords because they are going to use all combinations of numbers, special characters, and letters until the device is cracked. The biggest flaw with this technique is that it can take a ton of time to uncover the password.

3. Rainbow attacks—these are good for cracking any hashed passwords. The tool is really fast compared to others, but it is not able to uncover passwords that are more than 14 characters.

4. Keystroke logging—this is one of the best techniques for cracking a password because it is asking the targeted computer to basically send over the information. The hacker is able to place a recording device on the targeted system to take in all the keystrokes done on the computer. The information is then sent over using programs such as KeyGhost.

5. Searching for weak storages—there are a lot of applications in computers that will store the passwords locally, making them vulnerable to a hacker. When you have physical access to the computer, it is easy to find the passwords through text searches and sometimes they are even stored on the application.

6. Grab the passwords remotely—often it is not possible to physically access a system, it is still possible to get the passwords from a remote location. You will need to do a spoofing attack first, exploit the SAM file and have the information sent to you.

Once the hacker has access to these passwords, it is easier for them to get the information that they want. They can use the passwords to get onto the network, to get to emails, find out financial accounts, and so much more. You must remember that passwords are a huge vulnerability in your system and to figure out more secure ways to protect your system.

Chapter 6: Getting Through Internet Connections for the Hack

If you would like to work on hacking online, you will need to learn how to get through the internet connection, as well as the security features, that are found online. Here we are going to talk about how to hack through a WEP connection as well as how to perform an evil twin hack so that you can check to see if your system is susceptible to this kind of attack or not:

How to hack a WEP connections

While there are a few different types of internet connections that you can work with in order to hack, this is one of the easiest to go through. If this is the one that your system is working with, you will definitely need to run through a few tests to see if you have been hacked or if you can make it more secure. Some of the things that you will need to check and hack through a WEP connection includes:

1. To get started, load up the BackTrack and the aircrack-ng. you can fire up BackTrack and then make sure that it is plugged into the wireless adapter to see if it is running. You can type in lwconfi in order to see if this is working. The program is then going to tell you which of the adapter it can recognize and if this is working properly, it is going to see yours.
2. Then take the wireless adapter and set it so it is at promiscuous mode. This will allow you to see what other connections are available and you can type in "airmon-ng start wlano" in order to do this. You can then change the name of your interface to have it read momo. You now have the adapter inside of monitor mode and you can type in "airodump-ng mono" to see which access points are available and what is attached to them.
3. Start capturing your access point. You will need to pick which connection you want to get on and then capture it. You can do this by using the command

    a. Airodump-ng –bssid [BSSID of target] -c [channel number] -w WEPcrack momo.

    b. Once you enter this command, the BackTrack is going to start capturing packets fro the access point on the right channel. This will send the hacker all the packets that it needs in order to decode any passkeys that are present so they can get onto the wireless. However, it is important to realize that getting these packets will often take some time. If you need to get the packets quickly, it may be time to add in an ARP traffic.

4. Inject the ARP traffic—for anyone who doesn't want to wait around for the packets from WEPkey capture, doing an ARP packet and having it replay can help you get the packets that you need to crack the WEPkey. Since you already have the MAC and BSSID address from the target thanks to doing step 3, you will be able to use them to enter the following command:

   a. Aireplay-ng -3 -b [BSSID] – [MAC address] mono

   b. This will allow you to capture the ARPs through the access point of the target. You must keep going in order to capture the IVs that will come in as well.

5. Crack the WEPkey. Once you have the necessary amount of IVs in your WEPcrack file, it is time to run your aircrack-ng. Put in the command:

   a. Aircrack-ng [name of file]

   b. The aircrack-ng will enter the passkey in a hexadecimal format. You will just need to apply this key into your remote access point and then you are on the program. You can use it for free internet, to take over a computer on the system, and much more.

The Evil Twin Hack

The evil twin hack is an access point that will act like the access point that a user connects to, but it is manipulative. The target will just see their regular access point and think it is safe to get on, but this manipulative access point is used by a hacker to send the target to the hackers' premade access point, where the hacker can then start a dangerous man in the middle attack.

As a beginner hacker, you may need some practice doing the evil twin attack. Some basic steps to try out include:

1. Turn on BackTrack and start the program airmon-ng. Check to see if your wireless card is running properly by entering bt>iwconfig.

2. Once you have the wireless card, it is time to put it into monitor mode. You will be able to do this by entering the command bt >airmon-ng start wlano.

3. Now you need to fire up the airdump-ng. you will start capturing the wireless traffic that your wireless card is able to detect. To do this, enter

the command bt >airodump-ng mon0. After this step, you will have the ability to see all access points that are in range and can pick out the one that belongs to your target.

4. You will need to wait for when the target connects. Once the target gets onto the access point, you can copy the BSSID and the MAC address that you want to hack into.

5. Now the hacker will need to create an access point that has the same credentials.

   a. First, pull up a new terminal and type in bt > airbase-ng -a [BSSID] −essid ["SSID of target] -c [channel number] mon0

   b. This is going to create the access point that you want. It will look the same as the original access point so the target will click on it, but it puts the hacker right in the middle as the one in control.

6. De-authenticate the target—for the target to get onto your new access point, you will need to get them off the one they are connected to. Since many wireless connections will go with 802.11, everyone who is connected to the access point will be de-authenticated when you do this. When the target tries to get back on to the internet, they will connect automatically to the one with the strongest signal, which in this case will be your manipulated access point.

   a. To get the target off their access point, make sure to do the following command: bt > aireplay-ng −deauth 0 -a [BSSID of target]

7. Turn the signal of the evil twin up. The trick on this one is to get the fake access point to have a strong signal. It needs to be at least as strong, but preferably stronger, than the original point of access. This can be tricky because you are likely further away than the original access point.

   a. Iwconfig wlan0 txpower 27 will help you to turn up the signal on your access point.

   b. This can add 500 milliwatts to your power. If you are too far away though, this may not be enough. You either need to be closer to the target or consider a newer wireless card that is able to go up to 2000 milliwatts.

8. Put the evil twin to good use—once you have established the evil twin and you know that the target and the network are all connected to it, it is time to take the steps needed in order to detect all the activities going on in the system. It often depends on what you want to do with the system for where you will go from here.

Hacking: Top Online Handbook in Exploitation of Computer Hacking, Security, and Penetration Testing!

a. There are a lot of options of what to do at this point. Hackers who have gone and created an evil twin are interested in more than just free wireless so they will often do man in the middle attacks, intercept traffic, add in new traffic, or steal information from the system, often without the target realizing.

Conclusion

Working in the world of hacking can be really interesting. There are a lot of people who are interested in knowing how to protect their own systems from a hacker getting on and finding out information that they shouldn't, but most of us assume that going through the process of hacking is going to be too difficult to get started. But with the help of this guidebook, we are going to be able to learn some of the basics of working in hacking and how to protect your own network easily.

Inside this guidebook, we spent some time talking about the different ways that you are able to work with hacking. We started with some of the basics of hacking, such as the differences between white hat hackers and the black hat hackers and discussed how they often use some of the same methods to get things done. In addition, we talked about working on mapping your attack so that you have a plan and how to work with spoofing, man in the middle attacks, password hacks, and even how to hack through different connections online. All of these can come together to help you understand how to do a good hack and keep things safe from a hacker.

It is important that you learn how to keep your information safe from others who will try to get on your network and steal it. This guidebook is going to teach you some more about hacking and how you can use it for your needs and to keep your computer system safe.

www.ingramcontent.com/pod-product-compliance
Lightning Source LLC
LaVergne TN
LVHW052319060326
832902LV00021B/3986